CANADIAN
home&country

CANADIAN
COUNTRY STYLE

McArthur & Company
Toronto

CANADIAN
home&country

CANADIAN COUNTRY STYLE

TEXT BY JENNIFER DAVID   FOREWORD BY ERIN MCLAUGHLIN

First published in 2004 by
McArthur & Company
322 King St. West, Suite 402
Toronto, Ontario
M4V 1J2
www.mcarthur-co.com

Text: Jennifer David
Design: Alice Unger
Cover Photo: Donna Griffith

Library and Archives Canada Cataloguing in Publication

Canadian country style / Jennifer David, editor.

ISBN 1-55278-441-X

1. Interior decoration--Canada. 2. Decoration and ornament,
Rustic--Canada. I. David, Jennifer

NK1986.R8C36 2004   747'.0971   C2004-904190-8

The publisher would like to acknowledge the financial support
of the Government of Canada through the Book Publishing
Industry Development Program and the Canada Council for
our publishing activities. The publisher further wishes to
acknowledge the financial support of the Ontario Arts Council
and the Government of Ontario through the Ontario Media
Development Corporation's Ontario Book Initiative.

Printed in Canada by Transcontinental Printing Inc.

10 9 8 7 6 5 4 3 2 1

This book is dedicated to all those who yearn for the simple life, a place of quiet refuge and refreshment, and a meaningful, personable place to call home.

contents

foreword

My personal ideal of Canadian country style never seems as clear to me as when I am overseas. No matter where I am, I'm constantly reminded of Canada's raw and rugged beauty. Tuscany's sweeping views have fierce competition from the secret vistas I've found in Ontario's bucolic Mulmur Hills. And even the beaches on the south coast of England, with their magnificent limestone cliffs, don't inspire the same emotion as do the mystic red sands of Prince Edward Island. My personal experiences with the whimsical personality of Canada's countryside — often magical, sometimes dour — have helped to shape my sense of Canadian country style.

Throughout my home, I have surrounded myself with items and ideas that I love. Whether it's the wall of vintage mirrors I picked up at flea markets around the world or the shade of wall paint that reminds me of a room I slept in when I was a child, each detail has a story to tell, each connects with me in ways that are hard to define, yet the feelings evoked are very real. The magnificent places featured in *Canadian Country Style* share this unique trait — they have all been decorated with a sense of the homeowner's personal style, and that gives them their highly individual appeal.

In the chapters that follow, you can share in the inspiration taken from the pages of *Canadian Home & Country* magazine. I hope that some of these images will help you to create and feel confident in your own style. Though this book is divided into sections, don't be surprised if your tastes fit into more than just one. The beauty of Canadian country style is that, like the geographic and cultural distinctiveness of each of our provinces, we are able to mix and match what we love. If you're passionate about juxtaposing a rough-hewn scrubbed pine table with modern white Arne Jacobsen chairs, then you love the simplicity of urban country. But that doesn't mean you can't also mix in pretty touches of cottage style, like hanging a pair of vintage crystal chandeliers over that pine table. Have fun and be free with your decorating. Your Canadian country look should reflect your personal style, no matter where you live.

Erin McLaughlin

Erin McLaughlin
Editor, *Canadian Home & Country*

introduction

My journey with country style began with a table. It was more than 25 years ago and it was my first major furniture piece. In thinking about what I expected of a table, I knew that I wanted something that would be loved over the years as much as it was the day I bought it. I envisioned a table that would reflect the memories of meals shared, laughter and conversations enjoyed, homework toiled over and papers written. It had to be a well-built piece of furniture that could withstand daily use as a dining table, work surface, and surrogate desk, all the while gathering a pleasant patina. This brought me to my choice: a country antique. I now know it was a wise decision. That six-foot harvest table has withstood moves to our various homes, evolving décor, and three children. It's seen me through many business plans and set the stage for countless meals. And it's only improved with age. I love the table as much today as I did 25 years ago, and I'm sure as much as its former owners did.

I've come to learn from the talented editors, designers, and homeowners who have shared their stories and lives with us at *Canadian Home & Country* magazine that Canadian country style is indeed versatile and eclectic. It's probably our diverse heritage that has given us such a rich grounding for a distinctly Canadian country style. The homes you'll discover in our first book from *Canadian Home & Country*, with the visionary support of our book publishing partner McArthur & Company, all share common elements. They are nurtured by people who cherish the home as a place where friends and family gather, where dreams are made, and where anything is possible.

Jacqueline Howe
Publisher, *Canadian Home & Country*

preface

It's hard not to be drawn to the distinctive style and vitality of Canadian country design. Casual, inviting, and full of character, it conjures up images of picturesque retreats, places of sublime relaxation and peacefulness. Our modern country ideal symbolizes a simpler way of living — one that recalls the halcyon summer days of our childhood and evokes feelings of deep contentment and calm.

In an increasingly hectic world, Canadian country style has come to epitomize a lifestyle, one that represents a refuge from the breakneck pace of modern life. Indeed, the country-inspired interior is a sanctuary, offering warmth, integrity, a connection to the land and to our history, and an escape from the cares of the workweek. It respects tradition, and it allows us to feel closer to nature and to each other. It comforts and stimulates us, inducing us to kick-back and stay awhile. Few decorative styles are as creative, intimate, or unpretentious. Unlike our neighbours to the south, whose vision of country style is filtered through a patriotic lens, our varied cultural and geographic makeup leads to many interpretations. But at the heart of all country style is an unaffected charm and an inviting informality.

An eclectic medium, Canadian country style is above all about expressing who you are. Although it's difficult to point to one particular strain of country design as being the definitive Canadian style, there are several iconic elements that shape our perception. There's the Muskoka chair, so synonymous with cottage style, and Quebec's wealth of rustic pine antiques, now scattered across the country. There is the robust post-and-beam construction that reflects Western country personality, and the limestone exteriors that distinguish many country homes in Southwestern Ontario. In the melting pot that is Canadian style, these memorable country furnishings and finishes are as likely to show up in a cottage interior or urban bungalow as they are in a mountain retreat.

As the pace of life quickens, and the pressures to stay "connected" increase, the promise of a simple, unhurried, scenic getaway holds new appeal. On these pages you'll visit charming homes across the country, each a reflection of one of the nine distinctive styles we at *Canadian Home & Country* magazine believe embrace Canadian country style. There are those that demonstrate a traditional interpretation of country style and those that update the vernacular. There are those that borrow from other cultures, emulating a style with universal appeal, and others that have evolved naturally, stimulated by our impressive landscape and its rich offering of decorative inspirations.

There are cozy cottages that epitomize a free-spirited approach to décor, and chic urban dwellings that are, in essence, a little bit country. There are the rugged chalets and cabins that are shaped by a deep reverence for the Western landscape, with its majestic mountains and wide plains. There are homes and cottages whose interiors reflect the breezy elements found along the shores of our Atlantic provinces. And inevitably, there are the interiors influenced by our admiration for English and French country life, and tweaked to suit the Canadian climate and quality of light.

As diverse as these homes and their personable interiors are, they prove one thing. Whether Canadian country style is created deep in the heart of the countryside, perched by the side of a lake, overlooking the ocean, or in the thick of a teeming city, it has a distinctive attitude and enduring power to transcend time and place for all of those who live in its warm embrace.

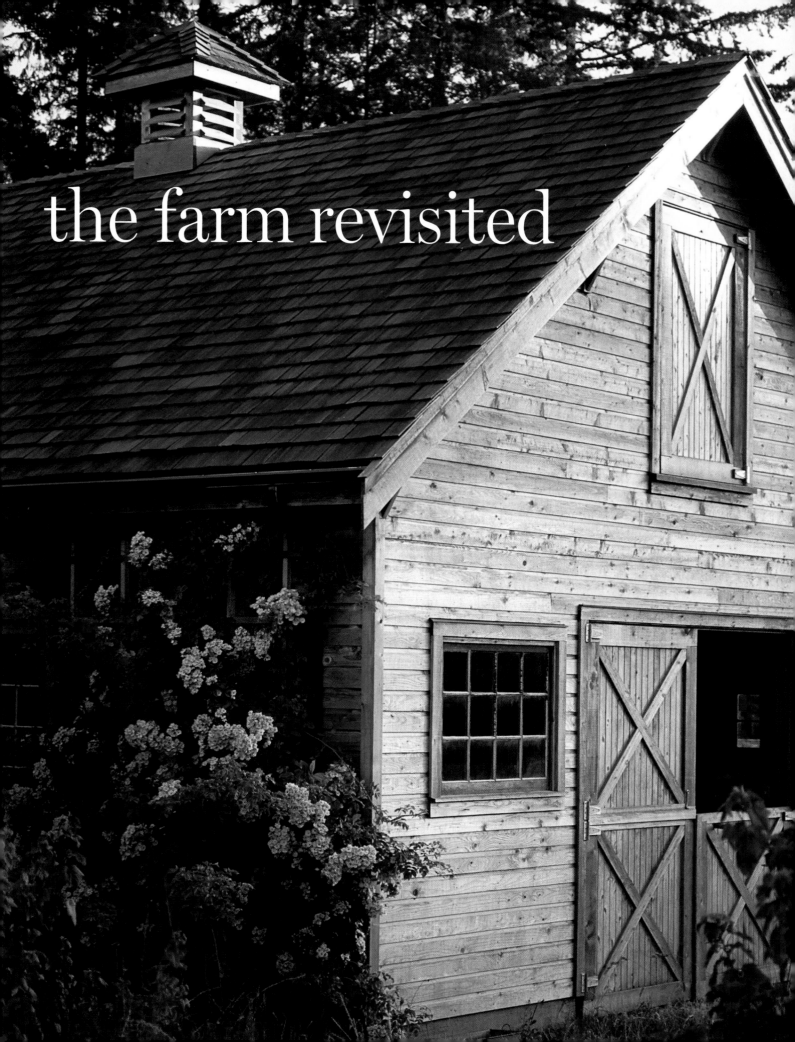

the farm revisited

The real roots of Canadian country style lie in our own rural past — in the simple structures that were home to the early agricultural pioneers and that still dot the countryside today. Planted firmly in the ground, surrounded by fields, trees, apple orchards, and rolling hills, the traditional farmhouse is the quintessential Canadian country abode.

The dictionary defines the farmhouse simply as "a house attached to a farm." And yet there's a great deal to be learned from this singularly unpretentious icon. It brings to life our history and common values in a way that few historians can. It speaks of a simpler time when environmental considerations shaped the way houses looked. It reflects the day-to-day lives of the people who lived in them — drawing attention to their hardships and suggesting their joy in communal celebration. It offers clues to their practical and adaptable nature. And its changing face traced the economic health and architectural fancies of the evolving Canadian scene, from humble rough-hewn structures to elaborate Victorian dwellings to newly renovated farmhouse retreats.

approach to accessories was typical.

The kitchen was the hub of farm life. A testament to self-sufficiency and long days of hard work, it was large, warm, and welcoming. If it seems familiar today, it's because so many of its features have been popularized in a variety of contemporary country styles: worn plank flooring, beadboard wainscotting, old hutches, glass-fronted cabinets, rustic hardware. A generous harvest table doubled as a work surface and a place to gather. Counter-to-ceiling windows, a mix of freestanding storage and furniture-like cabinetry with step-back cupboards, a beamed ceiling and open displays of equipment, cookbooks, and food in airtight containers pointed to an unaffected comfort that remains the cornerstone of the farmhouse look. A large porcelain farmhouse sink and utilitarian plate racks, staples of early farm life, are *de rigueur* again.

The key to the modern farmhouse look, and indeed to any country style, is an artful game of mix and match. To that end, the style blends beautifully with other modes of country décor. A display of retro ceramic storage jars on open shelving has both a classic farmhouse and urban country feel. A freestanding wood-burning stove is central to some cottage and Western cabin interiors and also to a farmhouse kitchen. A timeworn wooden table — a farmhouse signature — would not be out of place in any country kitchen — French or English, cottage or Acadian.

Just as the traditional farmhouse interior was a highly personal place designed to meet its inhabitants' practical needs, a contemporary farm-inspired décor blends individuality, comfort, and a healthy dose of rugged charm. It's authentic Canadian country style — without all the hard work.

Today, the farmhouse continues to be a source of rich inspiration for anyone looking to create a simple, unfussy atmosphere, whether it's in an actual farmhouse, a cottage, or an informal city home — wherever a little rustic authenticity is in order. The rooms of a typical early farmhouse were filled with pieces chosen for their function. Simple silhouettes, local materials, and solid craftsmanship trumped elaborate furnishings and fanciful fabrics. Sturdy, informal chairs, sofas, and tables evoked a lived-in, yet uncluttered comfort. Earthy colours connected the interior to the land. Honest, cheerful fabrics such as red-and-white gingham and hand-stitched quilts added dashes of colour. Family heirlooms such as intricate laces were cherished, if rare, indulgences. A restrained

(Previous page) This softly weathered barn is one of several old buildings clustered — European-style — around a central grove on a 10-acre property on Vancouver Island. (Opposite) Old-fashioned milk bottles from Vancouver's Avalon Dairy. (This page) A Toronto designer's country getaway features old-fashioned beadboard wainscotting in the kitchen, a classic backdrop for his collected furnishings and objects. A small bench displays spatter-ware bowls and two modern Italian bowls.

living

Simplicity and functionality have always been at the heart of farmhouse style. Traditional materials and craftsmanship, and a spare mix of upholstered and humble wood pieces, characterize the classic farm interior. But since there are no real rules to country decorating, evoking a mood is the main thing now.

(Opposite) A-turn-of-the-last-century farmhouse in Creemore, Ontario, boasts a wide-mouthed Rumford fireplace. The mantel holds a sweet display of delicate birds' nests. Classic farmhouse chairs can be drawn close to the fire on a cold day. (This page) In redecorating this weekend house, the owners created an eclectic look — one that would accommodate their existing furniture. Historic paint colours were used throughout; vintage children's toys add a note of whimsy.

(Opposite) An entryway, made cheerful with branches of forsythia, is pressed into service as additional storage. Luggage and blankets are tucked beneath the bench; striped pillows and vintage boxes rest on it. (This page) A typical old farmhouse mudroom features an indestructible stone floor, seating, and storage — overhead and in the bench. In a pinch, the unheated space doubles as cold storage.

the farm revisited

(Both pages) In an updated Ontario farmhouse, one of two walls that flanked the staircase was removed and replaced with the original banister, found languishing in the barn. The upholstered parson's chairs and seagrass carpet attest to the owners' contemporary sensibility. The view through the airy dining room and cozy living room overlooks the orchard just outside the window.

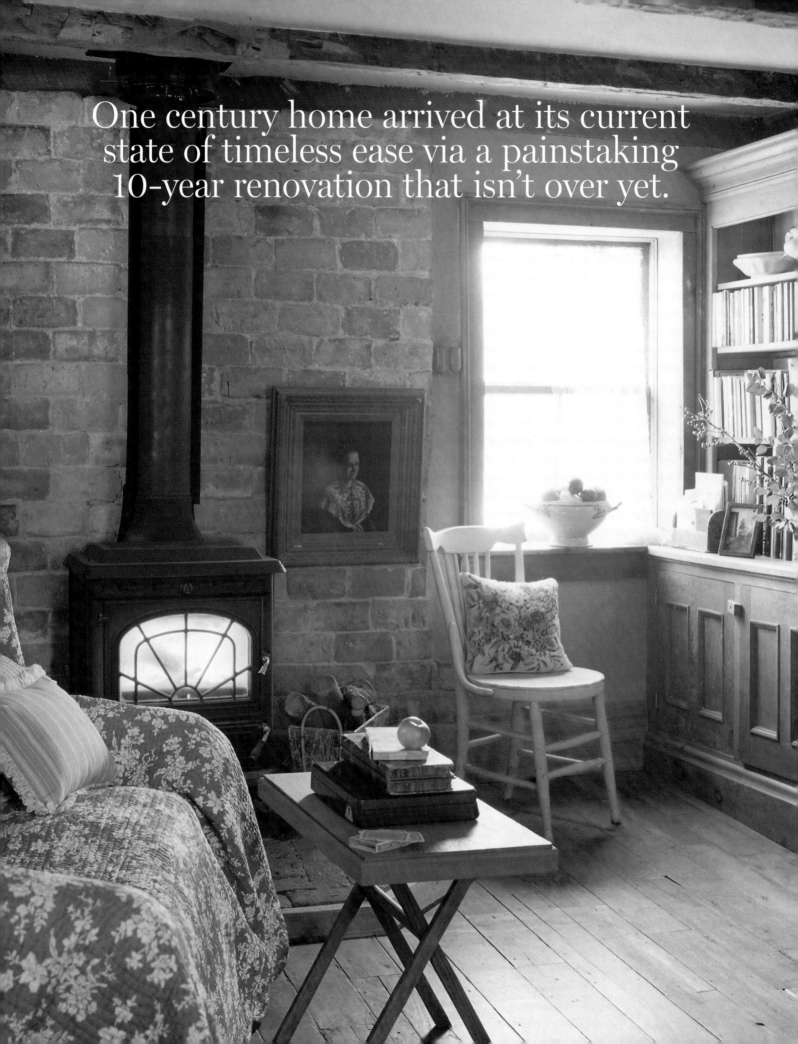

One century home arrived at its current state of timeless ease via a painstaking 10-year renovation that isn't over yet.

(Opposite) Brick walls, exposed beams, a wood-burning stove, muted tones, and a quilt thrown over a tired sofa are authentic rural touches. (This page) In typical farmhouse style, a Quebec armoire mixes it up with a Shaker-style table, Windsor chairs, and a collection of new and old pottery. Tin pails add colour and shine.

details

Transform a room with one or two striking antiques. • There's strength in numbers: display collections together. Stack quilts on a blanket box, line up spatter-ware bowls on an open shelf, and suspend an assortment of wicker baskets from the ceiling. • True farmhouse style is a bit of a mixing bowl — don't be afraid to blend pieces from different eras. Antiques and contemporary furnishings can coexist, as can distressed painted pieces and natural wood ones.

(Opposite) Though this circa 1830s farmhouse in P.E.I. has had several artful updates, the kitchen's pine floorboards are original. When the current owners purchased the house, the old dining set came with it. (This page) A pair of antique birdcages adds a note of playfulness into this old Paris, Ontario, kitchen while reinforcing the vertical pattern of the wainscotting. The print was picked up at a local shop.

(This page) Judging by the ingredients at hand, it's a safe bet that pie is on the menu. (Opposite) As part of a wholesale restoration, an East Coast kitchen dating to the 1790s was treated to several new features. A modern stove sits between cabinets designed and carefully "aged" with stain and fireplace soot to match one original to the room.

eating

The country kitchen is the hub of farm life. A source of warmth, hospitality, and down-home cooking, it's also an atmosphere worth emulating. Traditionally, an economical use of materials and utilitarian displays contributed to its ambience, but today it mixes primitive elements with sleek finishes and high-tech appliances. Practicality has always been the cornerstone of the farm kitchen.

the farm revisited

(This page, above) Additions to this 150-year-old kitchen include new cabinetry, a generous island, and new one-over-one sash-style windows modelled on the original ones. (Top) A pie cools in the sea breeze of Lunenburg Harbour. (Opposite) The concise U-shape of this kitchen may not be typically farmhouse, but several of its other features are, including wood plank flooring, a porcelain apron-front sink, and vintage metal accessories.

details

Add simple wood shelves to almost any kitchen style for additional display space. • Hang pots — French country-style — from the rafters. • Fit open shelves with woven baskets to store root vegetables, table linens, and cutlery. • Use cheerful red-and-white or blue-and-white checked and striped fabrics to dress windows and tables. • Start collecting everyday objects. Even the most modest mixing bowls or enamelware, for instance, can imbue a kitchen with classic farmhouse charm. • Install a porcelain sink.

rest

The quilt is at the heart of the country bedroom.
Handcrafted, using remnants of fabric, it epitomizes
the industrious, thrifty nature of farm living
while offering a creative and restful retreat from it.
The contemporary farm-inspired bedroom is
a spare and tranquil refuge in which a faded quilt
may be the strongest clue to its design heritage.

(Opposite) There's a utilitarian simplicity and sweet, old-fashioned appeal to these two bathrooms that draw inspiration from a common source: the farmhouse. (This page) Antique wrought-iron beds, picked up at a flea market, and French doors that open onto a balcony make this stylish master bedroom a favourite rereat.

(This page) A simple bedroom is a serene and summery refuge. (Opposite) A typically unadorned farm-inspired bedroom features a mix of old wooden pieces, a wicker chest, a candle lamp, and a farmhouse signature — a patchwork quilt.

In the timeless language of farmhouse style,
scatter rugs, quilts, and throw cushions
add texture, colour, and personality to a room.

details

Evoke a fresh farmhouse feel in the bathroom by introducing a claw-foot tub, a skirted pedestal sink, and beadboard wainscotting. • Install wall-mounted faucets for an old-fashioned touch. • If space allows, a weathered bench provides a rustic place to stack towels and display pretty soaps and other bathroom necessities. • Keep bedroom furnishings minimal for a restful atmosphere. One or two old pieces, such as a vintage spool or wrought-iron bed and a braided rug, will convey a country mood. • Layer quilts with a variety of patterned bed linens.

(Opposite) A renovated country bathroom mixes old and new to strong effect. The sleek trough-style sink is a reminder of farm living. (Left) It's an old trick, but a good one: a mirror at the foot of this antique tub enlarges the modest room. (Below) Foxgloves and peonies gathered from the garden add colour and fragrance to a tranquil bathroom.

northern light

Just as colour can be a dramatic decorating tool, so too can its absence. Fresh, airy, modern, and soothing, white is an ideal choice in any room designed for relaxation. Utterly serene, and easy to live with, it may just be the ultimate country colour.

There are so many reasons to choose white. In northern countries, ours included, it plays a unique role, introducing light during long, dark winters. It focuses the eye on architectural details and highlights the use of texture. It updates tired interiors and provides the ultimate backdrop for artwork and collectibles. It is the perfect foil for a laidback blend of contemporary elements and traditional country silhouettes. And more than any other colour, white lends a subtle drama to the line and form of chairs, sofas, tables, and decorative accessories.

In the city, where light is at a premium, stylish homeowners have long turned to white to create a feeling of brightness and space. And with good reason. White has an uncanny ability to expand a room, drawing light even into the dimmest recesses. In space-challenged city dwellings or country cottages, liberal doses of white introduce an enticing peacefulness and a sense of unhurried relaxation — the hallmarks of any great country interior.

Of course, there are those who reject all-white palettes for fear of creating rooms that appear austere rather than inviting. But rest assured. Few other palettes can compete when it comes to ensuring a tranquil atmosphere, particularly in a bedroom or bathroom — the two rooms we turn to for quiet reflection and a sense of luxurious comfort.

While dyed-in-the-wool modernists will have no trouble living in stark all-white schemes, the secret to living with white, at least for most of us, lies in mixing in other shades. Layering details in a range of subtly calibrated whites, or switching them for accessories in other tones — gentle or vibrant — instantly alters the personality of a room. Picture a striking all-white room where the only jolts of colour come from celadon-green and robin's-egg-blue blown-glass vessels and one or two colourful paintings; the effect is dazzling, and easily changed with a new group of accessories.

Far from being difficult to work with, white — and its companion range of pale hues — offers a surprisingly flexible backdrop against which virtually any colour or style can be layered. But for those brave enough to eschew colour in favour of this cool, clean palette, white is always right.

(This page) There's a stylish mix at work in this elegant Toronto home office. In a room dressed with off-white walls, a muted French Aubusson carpet, and a desk and chair of northern European extraction, a plush white faux-fur throw cushion becomes the lighthearted focal point. (Opposite) A classic white gift box needs little embellishment: a jaunty green-and-white gingham bow will do.

(This page) An urban townhouse living room adopts an updated English country outlook thanks to its relaxed tone-on-tone palette, spare splashes of colour, and one or two contemporary features, such as the black-and-white photographs and an empty, weathered white frame. (Opposite) An old-fashioned table, a ceramic baking mould, and fragrant hyacinths are unified by a restful white palette.

living

A subtle timeworn elegance comes from a soft white
scheme, especially when it's accented with painted
wooden pieces, slip-covered furnishings, and
second-hand finds, such as mirrors, that have been
treated to a warm-white wash. Cool, blue whites, on the
other hand, are evocative of contemporary settings.

In this pale and pretty living room in a
Quebec cottage, an occasional black accent
enlivens the gentle cream-and-lilac colour
scheme. A textured throw and sumptuous
silk draperies offer additional visual relief.

details

For a soothing atmosphere, use cool shades of greyed greens and blues against a creamy white background. • Transform a white theme with the addition of accents in a single bright colour — chartreuse, red, or robin's-egg blue. Change the accent shade, and the room transforms completely. • Use soft shades of white to harmonize a room filled with a mix of contemporary and traditional elements.

(Both pages) In this chic Montreal home, the artist owner's choice of warm-white walls and pale European antiques upholstered in a limited range of shades focuses the eye on the room's key feature: a striking pastoral painting.

The effect of adding one intense

(This page) Washable white slipcovers are a perennial — and practical — country staple. In this country getaway, flagstone flooring and a stone-and-iron side table are the only interruptions to the white-on-white scheme. (Opposite) A Swedish country table will blend in with any all-white atmosphere.

colour to an all-white theme can be spectacular.

details

Layer pastel shades with white. (Pastels work beautifully with white, largely because they are actually bolder colours that have been paled with shots of white.) • Energize an all-white space by adding a dazzling antique chandelier. • Paint walls white to provide a gallery-like backdrop for artwork and collectibles, to accent the line of furnishings, and to spruce up tired interiors.

(Opposite) This soothing combination of off-white, lavender, and green was inspired by the room's stained-glass window. (This page) The striking lines of three traditional Swedish chairs stand out all the more because they're white.

eating

The beauty of a white-on-white scheme in a kitchen or dining room is the opportunity it affords to showcase cherished collections of china, glassware, and pottery. Since there's no one shade of white, a variety of tones, or the addition of pale wall shades, seat cushions, or freestanding storage units will read as white while adding visual interest.

details

Add interest to an all-white room while keeping
the message consistent by including white
metal accessories and bleached or limed floorboards. • Use cushiony cork-rubber floor tiles in
soft shades to reinforce a pale mood. • Employ
baskets in a range of natural shades to store
napkins, tablecloths, flatware, and root vegetables.
• Update a flea-market table by cladding the
top in galvanized metal or stainless steel.

(Previous pages) A casual buffet showcases timeless glassware, ironstone, and silverware while a seasonal spray of flowers looks simply stunning. (Opposite) Kitchen implements — creamers, ladles, a sieve — are suspended over the island in a whimsical kitchen mobile. (This page) A porcelain apron-front, or farmhouse, sink is the focal point in this airy kitchen. Above, doors have been removed from the cabinets for an orderly display of glasses and dinnerware.

rest

Fresh, airy, and soothing, white is an ideal choice in any room designed for relaxation. It's utterly serene and easy to live with. Few palettes can compete when it comes to ensuring a tranquil atmosphere, particularly in a bedroom or bathroom — the rooms we turn to for quiet reflection and a sense of luxurious comfort.

(Previous pages) An inviting white-on-white bedroom layers tones and textures for a crisp, clean effect. A gauze corona adds a soft note of romance. (This page) A vintage-style faucet and showerhead imparts stylish personality to this new all-white bathroom in an old country house. (Opposite) A window ledge display demonstrates the ability of white to unify disparate objects.

details

Introduce a variety of textures, such as chenille, plush velvet, nubbly silk, and crisp linen, to soften a spare white bedroom. • Replace an old vanity with a clean-lined white pedestal sink — a country staple. • Keep floors bare to emphasize the lines of the room and the objects in it. • Install louvred shutters — a clean and classic window treatment. • In an all-white bathroom, or indeed any room, the injection of a single colour will have a profound effect. Try a few accents in a deep shade of orchid in the bathroom.

(Opposite, above and centre) A dreamy guest bathroom gains visual interest from its fluffy white bath mat, swagged shower curtains, and the juxtaposition of streamlined sconces and an old-fashioned mirror. (Below) An ottoman slipcovered in plush terrycloth and a stack of linen hand towels and pillows add a dash of luxury. (This page) A remodelled chaise — the skirt was removed and legs replaced — a charming French table, and a modern Flou bed come together beautifully in this restful room.

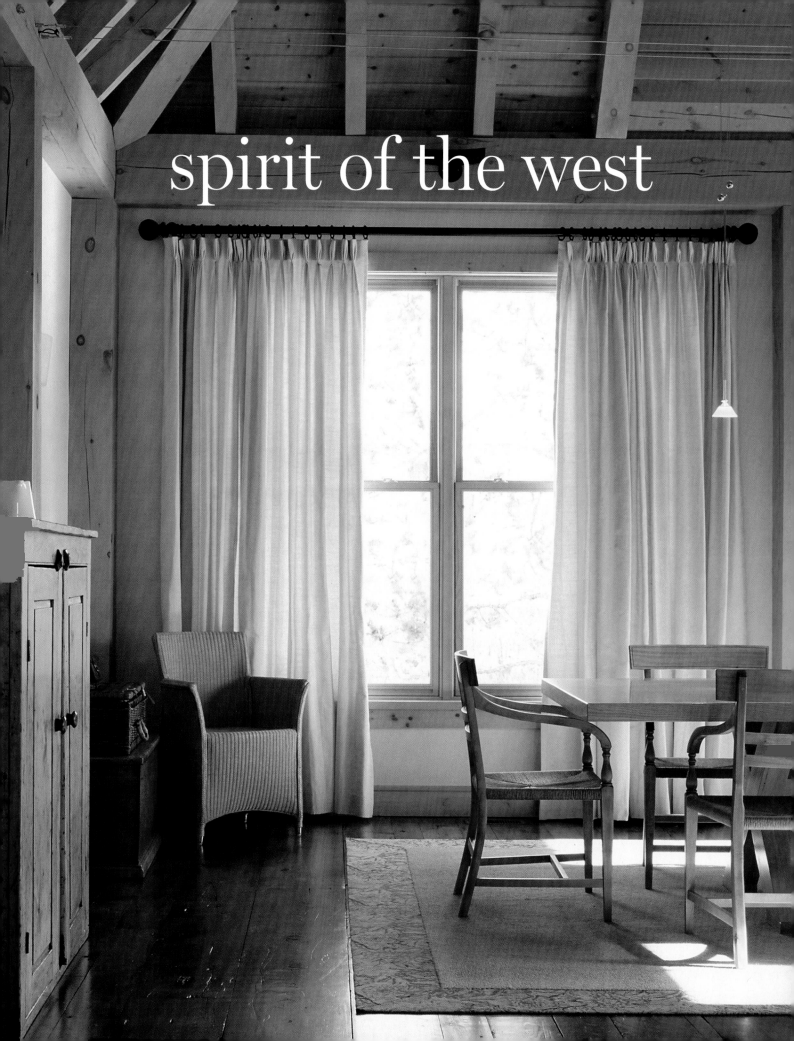

spirit of the west

In Canada's West, where towering mountains, tall stands of evergreens and hardwood, crashing surf, lush coastal rainforests, rich farmland, dusty ranches, and wide plains present a diverse landscape, country style is far more than a decorating trend. It's a way of life that has evolved from a unique relationship with the environment, a creative use of natural materials, and a desire to link the home to the land.

Of course there's more to the West than Alpine chalets and dude ranches — the ultimate Western clichés. Consider the island beaches and coastal towns dotted with seaside shacks and charming cedar-shingled cottages, or the lush, garden-filled cities where Tudor-style dwellings and one- and two-storey Craftsman homes intermingle with contemporary cement-and-glass structures. Think of Alberta's sprawling ranches, its mountain cabins, and the rugged frontier outlook that formed its cities. Picture Saskatchewan's treeless prairies, and its isolated farms and grain elevators.

There's an enormous variety of architecture in Canada's Western provinces, much of it influenced by American and British styles. And naturally, there's a wide range of interior approaches. The inclination to honour the dramatic setting, however, is a powerful one that cuts across stylistic and provincial barriers and is reflected in a bold use of rustic furnishings and indigenous materials, including basalt (a hard volcanic rock), bluestone, river rocks, granite, Western red cedar, and Douglas fir.

Indeed, nothing says Western country like an oversized stone hearth and the soaring beamed ceiling of a great room. Against the warmth and texture of these commanding elements, the décor requires a certain robustness. Relaxed leather sofas and plump club chairs, imposing log beds, twig side tables, birchbark-framed mirrors, native-inspired carpets, fabrics and art, and a few colourful accents act as counterpoints while reflecting nature's beauty. Decorative accessories may vary, but cowboy motifs, fur or cow-skin rugs, drawer pulls or lamp bases fashioned from antlers or horns, and wrought-iron lamps are central features that convey the mood.

The Arts and Crafts philosophy is strong in the West, too, where homeowners and designers still appreciate the movement's disdain for elaborate, mass-produced furniture. Utterly simple, well-constructed Mission-style chairs, tables, beds, chests of drawers, and lamps are beautifully suited to a more polished country atmosphere. In a rustic setting, they introduce a note of refinement.

One other influence is worth noting. Throughout the nineteenth and early-twentieth centuries, and again after World War II, large numbers of New Canadians emigrated from England and headed west in search of adventure. Many of the newly arrived English were drawn to cities such as Victoria and Vancouver, where a forgiving but decidedly soggy climate made them feel right at home, while the dramatic landscape heralded a new start.

As the English settled in, building new homes and lives for themselves, their interior style was informed by two key elements: the charming coziness of their traditional country heritage and a desire to respect the majestic natural beauty that surrounded them. In true country style, two worlds converged blending old and new with a desire for comfort and a strong connection to the landscape. And it created an all-new stylistic signature that had a sense of timeless charm and a deep reverence for the great outdoors.

(Previous page) An aura of warm simplicity prevails in this dining room, part of a large post-and-beam great room. Though much of the furniture in this weekend retreat is new, it was chosen — or in the case of the custom-made chairs, commissioned — to appear crisp, clean, and "country." (This page) Twig and wicker furniture — staples of Western country style — are recast in a refined armchair and desk.

living

The qualities that distinguish a Western country home — or one that's Western in spirit — are elemental: wood and stone harvested locally, colours and motifs drawn from nature, and a relaxed sense that you're getting away from it all, even if your home is far from the countryside.

(Opposite) The simple and striking furniture in this Vancouver great room was custom-designed to reflect the symmetry, scale, and clean lines of the new home's architecture. (This page) In the same house, a generous use of Douglas fir and bluestone and the casual, comfortable furniture inspired the home's designer, Lesli Balagno, to label it "West Coast meets Arts and Crafts."

In a large country house, a mix of tones and textures in one of several sitting rooms — this one designed for conversation or quiet contemplation — reinforces the home's relationship to its rural environment. The comfortable retreat has a light breezy feel in the summer and a cozy one in the winter.

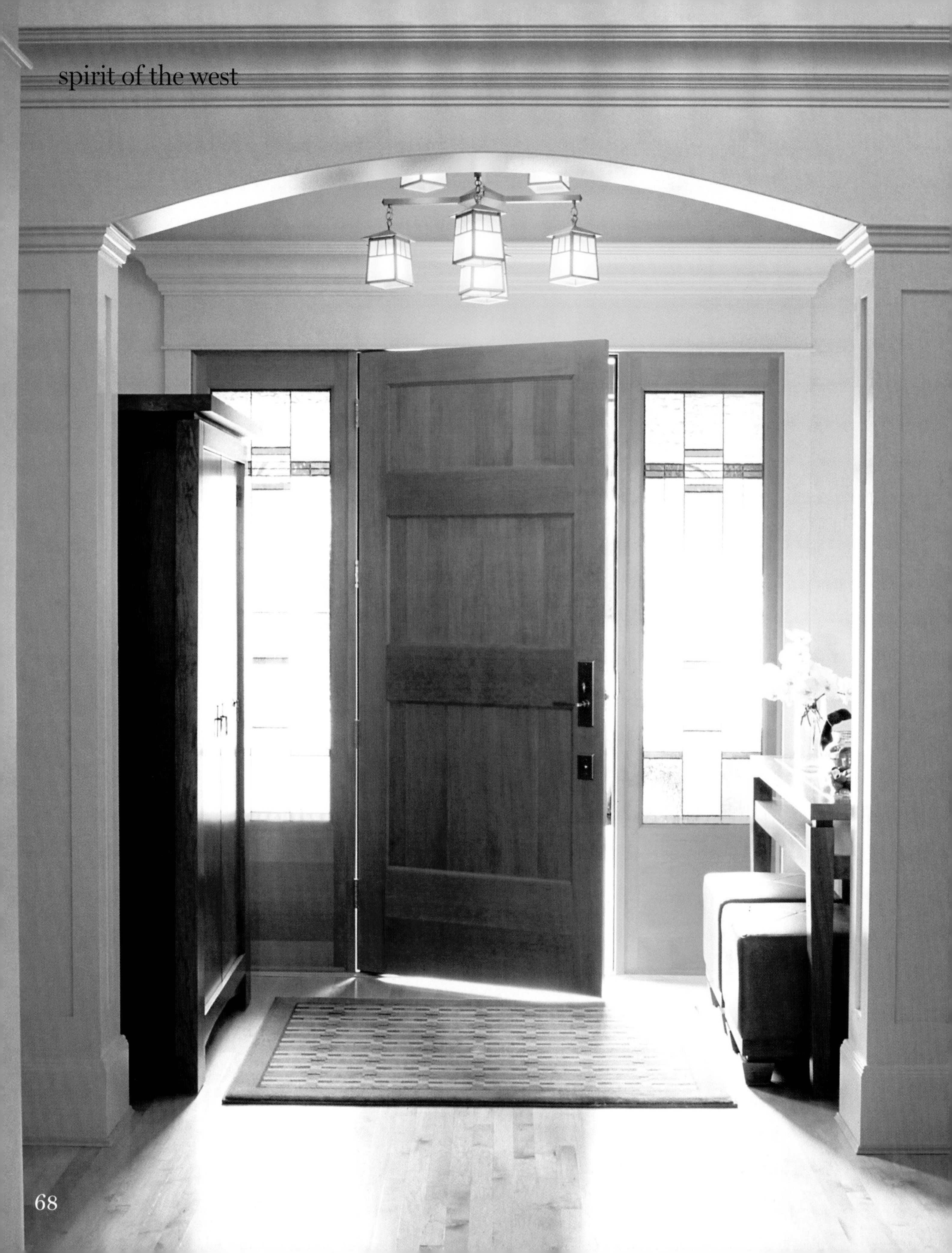

(Opposite) Several features of this inviting entryway hint at its Arts and Crafts inspiration, including the door with its stained-glass side panels and the light fixture. (This page) The vast scale of this great room is countered by a cozy arrangement of furniture. The red-toned Persian carpet, which is the basis for the room's décor, inspired the choice of brown leather sofas, red accents, and a collection of warm wood and wicker pieces.

(This page) Balance is the secret to the appeal of this charming tableau, featuring an old butler's table, an antique map of Quebec City, and a contemporary lamp. (Opposite, top to bottom) Weathered items, found objects, and textured pottery create a casual country arrangement. Sitting atop the old Quebec pine sideboard is a trio of pebble-glazed bowls and a ceramic jug. An assortment of pressed-glass water goblets creates a sparkling still life.

details

Resist the temptation to over-decorate. Collections built over time have the most natural appeal. • Employ muted greens and reds to suggest a woodland retreat. • For a polished atmosphere, consider adding Arts and Crafts–style furnishings. • Reduce the scale of a room by grouping furniture in cozy arrangements. • A true mountain getaway requires storage for outdoor gear: outfit an entryway with ample hooks, racks, shelves, and a comfortable place to sit.

eating

As with the rest of the Western country home, the kitchen and dining room have a sense of natural style and ease, essential ingredients in a home designed as a retreat. Even if they're far removed from the big skies, mountains, and open fields that inspired them, they are friendly, relaxed, and full of warm, tactile ingredients.

(Opposite) Leaded-glass windows, a display of hanging pots, and traditional cabinetry signal the English heritage of this West Coast country kitchen. (This page) The whitewashed stone walls and wooden cabinet in this uncluttered dining room allow the artfully aged Windsor-style chairs and generous harvest table to take centre stage.

(This page) In this renovated country kitchen, stainless steel appliances and a granite countertop are contemporary foils for its rustic aspects. (Opposite) The earthy colours and textures of this old Ontario farmhouse are vintage Western style. A collection of salt-glazed pottery from Salt Spring Island adds interest to a shelf fashioned from an old barnboard.

details

Use stone veneer on an interior wall to bring the look of the great outdoors in. • Combine natural elements with warm colours to achieve the look of an old house. • Display handmade pottery from a local artisan for visual interest and texture. • Recycle old floorboards for an instantly authentic look. • Introduce copper accents, such as pendant lights, for a note of warmth against stone walls and stainless steel appliances.

rest

Everyone needs a room
of her own — a refuge where
personal tastes and desires
count for more than the
comfort of others. It should
be a place of heightened
sensuousness, quiet solitude,
and peaceful relaxation.
The Western spin on this
sybaritic notion of bed and
bath incorporates one or
two hand-crafted elements
and the sense that nature is
never very far away.

(Opposite) A pine piece, outfitted with a Carrara marble countertop, a sink, and faucet, makes for a cabinet with character. The mirror echoes the home's natural setting. (This page) In a restful bedroom, a generous use of natural wood is balanced by off-white bedding and a jovial red quilt. The overall effect is one of harmony — perfect for a good night's sleep.

(Opposite) This serene yet stylish bathroom offers subtle clues to its Western setting, including an effective use of Douglas fir in the cabinetry and mirror trim, a natural colour scheme, and a tailored Arts and Crafts mood.

details

Use subtle colours inspired by nature (soft greens, whites, and faded pinks) to echo the blooms and foliage of the Western environment. • For an airy take on Western country, juxtapose white slipcovered furniture with a fieldstone fireplace. • Leave trim work unpainted for a casual note of warmth. • In the bathroom, embrace the view — even if it's of your own backyard — by installing a claw-foot tub beneath large casement windows.

new england

There's no denying the profound influence of English interior design on our Canadian country scene. Perhaps more than any other ideal, it's English country life, with its storied pleasures — from gardening to horseback riding to long country ambles — that serves as cheerful inspiration in our own country homes.

Canadians have long had affection for the traditions of English country life. We have adopted many of its beloved decorating traits, especially antiques and time-honoured furniture shapes, such as the ever-popular William Birch sofa. Modern city-dwellers might even be surprised to learn that their homes contain traces of English country style — in details that are often not associated with the country house, but which did indeed originate there. Contemporary slipcovers and eccentric collectibles, for instance, are English country in nature (slipcovers are an eighteenth-century invention developed to protect upholstery fabrics from soot). Familiar English country imports include fabric, wallpaper, fine

china, and colours inspired by nature. Flagstone floors, brick walls, and classic fabrics of cotton, silk, and wool are traditional elements we've been only too happy to borrow. Leaded windows, cozy unfitted kitchens, and profusions of flowers recall charming thatch-roofed English cottages, while impressive entrances, panelled walls, ancestral portraits, and glass conservatories are more to-the-manor-born.

The key to the English country look has always been a feeling of timeless comfort and relaxation, an atmosphere created by a casual (and in Victoria's day, cacophonous) mix of colour and pattern and easy-to-live-with collections of old furnishings and antiques. (As one Toronto designer is fond of pointing out, no English country atmosphere is complete without a French antique

or two.) Welcoming entranceways and mudrooms serve the country house well and are practical ideas suited to our own messy climate.

There's also an unmistakable lodge sensibility to some English country homes that strikes a chord in Canada. Exposed beams, stone walls, oversized fireplaces, and floor-to-ceiling windows embrace the outdoors and are popular features that have all been integrated here, particularly in the West.

So what of the glazed chintzes, formal, overstuffed rooms, and dark ancestral portraits that are so much a part of the English country cliché? Oh, they're still around, to be sure. But in recent years, a new country style has emerged, casting off its musty old reputation in favour of a relaxed brand of charm, a remarkable attention to balance and detail, and an enticing combination of comfort and elegance. Now at the forefront of international décor, and warmly embraced here in Canada, English country style combines a deep sense of tradition, an artful approach to fabrics, colour and pattern, and liberal doses of whimsy. It takes the best traditional style, blends it with a pared-down approach, and throws in some quirky charm for a refreshing vision that can only be called New England.

(Previous page) The entrance to a handsome
country house is quietly welcoming. (Opposite)
From the spacious stone terrace of a new
rural Ontario house, the owners can enjoy
the view. (This page) English country's new
attitude is reflected in an uncluttered sitting
room. A nosegay, suspended upside down
on the wall, is a whimsical nod to tradition.

living

The first rule of English country's revitalized look is that there are no rules. Floral fabrics still abound, as do traditional furniture forms and flagstone floors. But now the fuss is gone. Colours are brighter, patterns are bolder, and textures are softer.

(Opposite, left) Leaning insouciantly against a wall, a meticulously restored gilt mirror reflects the light that pours in the window opposite it. (Opposite, right) An absence of strong colour gives this pretty country dining room a fresh formality. The chandelier is a whimsical addition. (This page) A relaxed mix of yellow florals and red-and-white checks on throw cushions relate to each other and to the subdued furnishings in this comfortably appointed living room.

85

(This page) A secluded alcove at the foot of the stairs is the perfect spot for a quiet read. At night, the daybed, which doubles as a window seat, can accommodate overflow guests. (Opposite) A French influence is felt in the fabrics in this simple country scheme. A charming jug holds a single stem of lily of the Nile (*Agapanthus*).

(Opposite) Designer Sarah Richardson's version of English country style includes a touch of paisley in the throw cushions, a French walnut armoire faced with chicken wire, and a pared-down take on the traditional William Birch sofa with its rolled arms and show-wood legs. (This page) In a room full of quiet colours and subtle textures, Richardson introduces warmth and character with a range of wood tones and displays of family pictures and quirky collections, such as the antique army dumb bells.

(This page) Traditional fabrics, mostly from Laura Ashley, and an elegantly eclectic mix of furnishings give this guesthouse in rural Ontario an English country spin. (Opposite) If there is one fabric house that has helped shape the English country aesthetic, it is Colefax and Fowler. Founded in 1934 by Lady Sibyl Colefax and iconic designer John Fowler, the company's delicate embroidered fabrics, loose-weave linens, and exquisite floral fabrics are classic but never stodgy.

details

Use natural stone flooring in an entranceway. It's practical, beautiful, and designed to withstand our sloppy weather. • Evoke an English country mood by mounting patterned plates on a wall. • Include cherished objects — quirky collections or walnut-framed family pictures — throughout the house. • Pretty patterned slipcovers — an English invention — create instant atmosphere.

eating

Duplicating the inviting aura of an English country kitchen isn't difficult. Introduce comfy seating, whether it's around a farm-style table or a shabby-chic sofa. Combine fitted and unfitted elements, and open displays of china, glassware, and linens for a practical charm. And last but not least, put on the kettle . . .

A weekend retreat in the Ontario countryside has a singularly English attitude that gains strength from traditional cabinetry, comfortable seating (including an inviting window seat), a mix of striped and floral accents, open displays of cookbooks on the window ledge, and a generous farmhouse sink.

COFFEE

SUGAR

FLOUR

93

details

Evoke English country style in the kitchen with a
porcelain farmhouse sink and built-in plate racks.
• Introduce character to a fitted kitchen with
open displays of kitchen implements, cookbooks,
glassware, and mixing bowls. • Inject a casual
note of practicality by installing a butcher-block
surface, either in an island or by replacing a
section of countertop. • Set a relaxed tone by
drawing mismatched chairs up to a kitchen table.

(Opposite, above) A fanciful chandelier, pretty table linens, and drapery fabrics dress up the eating area in an informal country kitchen. (Below) A striking pewter collection and charcoal-grey library pulls complement the cool tones of this traditional cabinetry. (This page) A practical combination of work surfaces — wood, tile, and stone — and fitted and unfitted cabinetry characterize this compact kitchen. Displays of pretty china, glassware, linens, and mixing bowls put everything within reach.

rest

Private, comfortable, calm, uncluttered. The ideal country bedroom is a place of sublime refuge. Its serene atmosphere induces relaxation, while its design makes room for personal whims and indulgences. Restrained displays of personal touches — silver brushes, frames, mirrors, a small vase of fresh-picked flowers — reflect the details we love about new and traditional English country style.

Details are important in a room
with few embellishments. Plain
white bed linens focus the eye
on the charming antique bed.
A red-patterned rug adds warmth
to an otherwise cool scheme.
A pretty blue-and-white country
border plays up the ceiling's angle.

(This page) The dark, curvy contours of this dramatic antique bed contrast nicely with the timeless white linens. A sweet vase of roses picks up on the room's other country touches. (Opposite) Though some of its elements are clearly French, including the quilted bedding, the overall effect in this airy, eclectic bedroom is English. The unexpected use of collectibles — such as the birdcage — adds a note of playfulness.

(This page) In an updated master bathroom, the built-in tub surround creates practical storage, while a limited palette ensures a restful mood. The tub fits snugly under the window, where bathers can gaze at the view. (Opposite) A Victorian-style hand-held showerhead is side-mounted to ensure comfortable bathing.

An atmosphere that induces pure relaxation
is the greatest luxury of all.

details

Ensure an airy mood of calm by minimizing clutter. • Limiting the palette in the bedroom and bathroom will keep the atmosphere restful. • Balance colour and pattern with some spare details — an uncovered floor or sisal carpet — in order to keep the look fresh. • Use antiques — beds, mirrors, rugs — to anchor the room. • Rotate restrained displays of personal collections and family heirlooms, such as sterling silver combs and brushes and childhood mugs.

(Opposite) In true bed-and-breakfast style, the sink in this guest bedroom gives visitors a measure of comfort and privacy. A mix of Laura Ashley fabrics and a simple slipcover underscore the English country attitude in this rural Ontario cottage. (This page) Even the smallest sleeping nook is enticing when it blends luxurious bed linens, a splash of colour and pattern, and a place to rest your books.

JANE URQUHART

THE UNDERPAINTER

urban country

Torn between two decorating worlds, unable to commit to an undiluted country atmosphere or a sleek, sophisticated city vibe? Not to worry. The most contemporary, and in some respects captivating, of Canadian country styles seems to be both of the city, and a respite from it. The urban country interior exhibits an intriguing interplay of old and new, of cool spareness and primitive warmth, of ultramodern furniture and country antiques. In this gentle game of give and take, the harmonious but personable décor rises above location and architectural character to make its own playful statement.

This is easily the edgiest of country decorating schemes. An unfussy but friendly fusion, it borrows elements from the traditional country home and makes them work with urban architecture and modern furnishings — happy news for the burgeoning ranks of condo-dwellers. At its best, the Canadian urban country home is modern and classic at the same time. It draws inspiration from our own country scene, with its farmhouse and cottage references, and from the world of sleek international design.

Take the kitchen, for instance. Chances are it has a largely unfitted appeal, eschewing cookie cutter cabinetry in favour of a mix of classic country-style storage cabinets and armoires and contemporary pieces. For warmth and character, it may feature at its heart a distinctive Aga cooker (an English country staple that is now available here), a large porcelain apron-front sink — a reminder of those found in old farmhouses — open shelving to display prized collections of pottery or glassware, and a comfy sofa. It may also have sleek stainless steel appliances, the latest retro-style faucet, and an industrial pendant light. In the dining area an assemblage of modern chairs, such as Arne Jacobsen's bent plywood Series 7 masterpieces or Italian designer polypropylene chairs, might cozy up to an ample harvest table. The effect is at once warm, welcoming, and strikingly eclectic.

In the living room, too, many of the details may evoke a country mood. A rustic antique pine box might serve as a coffee table in a tailored setting. Old-fashioned wicker chairs may share floor space with a clean-lined, contemporary sofa. Sumptuous silk fabrics in casual stripes and plaids can soften the windows, and throw cushions add colour and interest to an otherwise neutral backdrop. Warm wood elements, possibly even rough-hewn, will stand in striking contrast to the crisp shapes and chrome legs of sleek sofas, chairs, and low-lying coffee tables.

Keeping rooms uncluttered, with a minimal number of colours, will enhance a mood of airy calm. But the real appeal of this fresh and enduring country style is the space it leaves for personal expression. Start with the objects you love best, don't be afraid to mix them up, and whatever you do, don't rush it. The best interiors take time.

(Previous page) There's a pleasing tension to this new country tableau that pits warmth against timeless simplicity. Striking black-and-white photography updates any environment. (Opposite) A leather banquette cushion and chic pendant light are the modern counterpoints in this Vancouver kitchen. (This page) Rustic wicker chairs and a weathered side table hold their own in a sophisticated setting.

living

The look of urban country is fresh, unfussy, and intriguing. It combines modern design with traditional materials, mixes warm country elements with cool urban architecture and modern furnishings, and marries minimal features to gracefully aged surroundings.

(Opposite) An antique wooden chest — the home-owner's childhood toybox — and modern art are the focal points in this comfortable sitting room. (This page) Victorian architecture plays host to an attractive assortment of family antiques, contemporary furnishings, and carefully chosen collectibles.

A house can be classic
and modern
at the same time.

Tailored furniture complements the traditional cabinetry and pared-down fireplace in this updated Vancouver home. The funky, cow-skin upholstered stools at the coffee table were designed for the daughter of the house.

An artful mix of modern, vintage,
and antique pieces epitomizes urban
country in this stylish century home.

details

Urban country is an understated look: aim for flexible, neutral tones and simple silhouettes — and err on the side of minimalism. • Keep your rooms uncluttered by rotating displays of objects and collections. • Keep wood tones consistent, and you can mix styles of furniture without it looking untidy. • Minimize your colour palette for a mood of airy calm.

eating

The urban country kitchen combines the best of modern and traditional design. It updates the classics by juxtaposing them with fresh new features. Think Shaker-style cabinet doors, porcelain apron-front sinks, minimal upper cabinetry, open displays of china and pots, neutral tones, a mix of counter surfaces, and sleek contemporary chairs.

(Both pages) Even a tiny apartment kitchen can blend style and function. Here, a butcher-block counter doubles as work surface and breakfast bar. Freshly painted Shaker-style cabinetry is the classic foil for the room's vintage details, including an apron-front sink, library pulls, and checkerboard floor. The charcoal-grey walls and stainless steel appliances are strictly modern. (Opposite, far left) The pantry, which is visible from the adjoining dining room, displays a collection of heirloom china.

details

Choosing a common theme for china — such as white or textured patterns — will unify different styles, making for a harmonious display. • A well-balanced urban country kitchen benefits from timeless finishes, such as marble or slate countertops, painted wood, and Shaker-style cabinetry. • Make room for personal flourishes. Open displays of prized pottery or other collectibles will bring colour and life to a clean-lined kitchen or dining room.

(This page) Gleaming appliances, cement countertops and fresh white paint — all hallmarks of the modern kitchen — play well against the custom wood cabinetry, poured glass tiles, and mottled-glass-front upper cabinets in this meticulously recreated Craftsman kitchen. An industrial gas range is contemporary and practical. (Opposite) Period-perfect details include vintage pendant lights and old hot-water rads that have been stripped and nickel-plated.

(This page) Nothing says country like crisp white beadboard and Shaker-style doors. They distract the eye from the room's more contemporary but practical features: a sleek cooktop, stainless steel dishwasher, double ovens, and twin sinks. A black cherrywood countertop and the occasional shot of apple green on the walls warm the all-white scheme. (Opposite) In this lakeside retreat, two views of an open kitchen/dining room show its sophisticated but timeless feel and flexibility as an entertaining space.

rest

Creating a retreat that's modern and country fresh at the same time means keeping it simple. Settle on a soothing colour scheme, layer luxurious bed linens, focus on generally soft lighting (but don't forget a good light for reading), and go easy on the accessories.

(This page) This room's bisque-coloured walls, all-white bed linens, and lack of adornment make for an ultimately relaxing environment. The weathered door is a rustic grace note; the tubular stair rail underscores the room's dual personality. (Opposite) By rotating personal mementoes you can introduce a whole new look to a simply decorated room.

Creating an oasis of calm can be as simple as paring down your furnishings, throwing on a few coats of paint in a restful shade, and dressing the bed in layers of white. Here, old school desks stand in for bedside tables and visually widen the space. The lamps make a modern statement, and point the eye to the room's pleasing focal point: a treasured piece by Toronto artist Cybèle Young.

(This page and near right) Two completely different bedside vignettes combine traditional and modern accessories to strong effect. (Opposite, above) Inspired by oversized colour-saturated photographs of peonies, designer Sarah Richardson infused this whimsical country bedroom with a fresh colour scheme. A luxurious twill-covered chaise and pillow-strewn bed (below) invite repose. Splashes of bright pink add definition

details

Create a mood of calm by bathing the bedroom in gentle light. • If space allows, have a place — other than the bed — to curl up in, such as a cushy chair and ottoman, a chaise longue, or a window seat. • Replace a bedside table with a stack of old suitcases, a wicker basket, or an old stool. • Choose classic furnishings, such as a sleigh bed, that convey warmth and comfort. • Use a country armoire to gracefully conceal linens or electronics — even a home office. • If the space is small, limit the number of accessories on display.

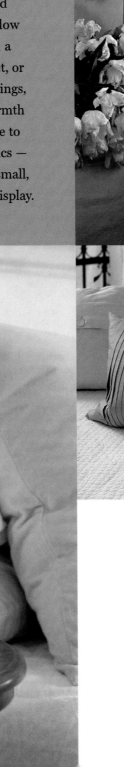

Details play a pivotal role in creating the right mood

In this muted, and ultimately soothing scheme, the "colour" comes from the furniture's warm walnut tones and some intriguing and harmonious decorative accessories. Despite the room's apparent lack of contemporary features, its calm, uncluttered atmosphere and crisp bed linens give it a modern demeanour.

acadian style

In the Maritime provinces, and scattered throughout Quebec, there is a distinct design heritage that can be traced back through the centuries to one of the more regrettable chapters in Canadian history. It's an expressive style marked by simple furniture forms, natural saturated colours, dark wood elements, and ever-present maritime touches. Rooms are uncluttered, even lean, with a look reminiscent of the colonial aesthetic. Warmth is derived from the familiar comfort of hooked rugs, quilts, and one or two colourful accents.

In the traditional Acadian interior, rustic touches are balanced by a subtle air of refinement. Antiques, the occasional touch of lace, and imported carpets and fabrics are countered by rudimentary painted wood pieces and utilitarian displays of crockery, glassware, and pewter. Trim work cast in historic shades of blue, red, and green appear all the more dramatic against off-white walls. Boldly individual and strikingly direct, contemporary Acadian-style décor hints at the proud and unique culture of the pioneers for whom it is named. Theirs is a tragic story, but one that goes a long way toward explaining their passionate attachment to hearth and home.

The original Acadians were a community of one hundred families, mostly farmers from different regions in France, who emigrated early in the seventeenth century. Settling first around Le Have and then moving to the Bay of Fundy, they farmed, fished, and generally sought to establish themselves in independent communities based on family, faith, and their common language. They were determined to maintain a neutral and, to borrow a contemporary phrase, *distinct society*. So they isolated themselves from the political manoeuvres of the French and English as land changed hands up and down the Eastern Seaboard.

When they refused to swear allegiance to the British crown in the 1750s, the English acted swiftly and harshly. They forcibly expelled more than six thousand Acadians, burning their homes, and scattering families to the wind. Some Acadians fled to Quebec, some died, and some hid among the Mi'kmaq. Others were imprisoned or returned to France. But most were deported south to the colonies, where they were hardly welcomed and rarely understood. The lucky ones made it as far as Louisiana, where a receptive French community took them in.

But that wasn't the end of the resilient Acadians. Although the *grand dérangement* lasted eight years, eventually the exiles were allowed to return. Those who could, made their way back to Acadia — to land now known as Nova Scotia and New Brunswick, where their descendants continue to live and celebrate their unique roots.

Today, throughout the East Coast and well into Quebec lie significant clues to the original Acadian style, the essence of which can be seen in a typically spare blend of French and maritime influences. Antique pieces are important, but rarely ornate. Colours, particularly deep shades of red, green, and blue, accent the proliferation of natural materials and details: stone hearths, hand-hewn wooden beams, and wide-plank flooring. Weathered dressers and cabinets (in various states of distress) contain kitchen overflow; stoneware — a staple of the Acadian kitchen — is displayed on open shelves. Simple wooden chandeliers hang above casual country tables. Hooked rugs decorate floors and walls, and convey their maker's heritage.

It's been four hundred years since Canada's earliest pioneers arrived in Acadia, and two hundred and fifty years since they were forced from it, but their energetic and humble emphases on the comforts of home resonate still.

(Previous page) Simple lace curtains hanging in the window of this shingle-sided cabin — a converted milk house — hint at the charmingly rustic atmosphere within. (Opposite) A colander of crimson berries picks up the quintessential Acadian accent colour. (This page) The juxtaposition of vivid trim colour and off-white walls is another bold signature.

living

The traditional Acadian
home reflected the heritage
and skill of its inhabitants
and the resources of
their new land. Capturing
the essence of this
unique and comfortable
style requires a taste
for simple country antiques,
restrained arrangements
of furniture, bold colour,
and natural materials.

A sensitive and meticulous restoration of this eighteenth-century home in Lunenburg, Nova Scotia, revealed the living room's original crown moulding, now painted a historic shade of blue. A newly assembled collection of antiques gives the room character. The rug is a souvenir from the owner's travels in Dubai.

(This page) The clean lines of this low-key living room, with its lively red accents, roomy armoire, and ships on the mantel, echo Acadian style. (Opposite) Disparate objects, sparely arranged, demonstrate how easily a mood can be evoked. The mahogany plantation bed is an American antique and the birdcage Windsor armchair hails from Ontario, but the painted trim, deep colours, and genteel simplicity of the room all suggest Acadia. Note how even the most unassuming arrangement of flowers softens formal furnishings.

(Opposite) There's a relaxed air of eclecticism in the living room of this suburban Montreal home. The warm colour scheme, mix of patterns and textures, and generous stone fireplace add character. As the sofa's seat cushions faded with wear and tear, the owner reupholstered them in rich brown leather. (This page) The home's accent colour is echoed in this striking vase of *Ilex* branches.

137

Early pieces of furniture

(Opposite) In a quiet corner of a living room, simple country antiques create a rustic but airy "office." The trim work, painted a custom shade of Louisbourg-style green, and the rich tone of the wood pieces add visual warmth to the room. (This page) A Shaker-style pegboard brings order to the master bedroom.

immediately convey another era.

(Opposite) Saying they give her a "sense of belonging," the owner of this country house displays edited collections of antique objects — some of them unearthed during the home's painstaking restoration. (This page) It took the home-owner a year to strip the living room's wainscotting and wood trim before she painted it a period green. Her husband, an accomplished carpenter, rebuilt the staircase (below).

details

Forego off-white trim and wood panelling in favour of a historic shade. It adds instant character to a room. • Keep arrangements of furniture lean. • Resist the temptation to restore all wooden pieces. Traces of old paint — and other signs of distress — make furnishings appear friendly, even fresh. • If antiques are out of reach, collect sturdy, simple pieces that serve a purpose — an armoire or a storage cupboard, for instance.

eating

The early Acadians had a strong sense of family and community. And being French, they enjoyed their food. The sharing of informal meals around a casual harvest table in the warm glow of a roaring fire is a timeless pleasure, and one that recalls the rustic Acadian *joie de vivre*.

(Opposite) In this newly decorated dining room, reproductions of farmhouse furniture, such as maple comb-back chairs in a black vintage paint finish, a pine harvest table, and a candlelight chandelier, as well as the deep red tone of the walls and fabrics, recall Acadian style. (This page) Sometimes even the smallest details — simple bistro glasses, or a vintage-style faucet, for example — impart a strong sense of style.

143

(Left) Even an artfully restored colonial-style cottage benefits from a few modern touches, including new subway tiles and stainless appliances and countertops. And yet the overall effect is still authentically aged — note the wide floorboards, collections of stoneware and pewter, and simple wooden bowls and tray. (Above) The impact of a few old pieces — a milk bottle, mismatched water goblets — is strong if you keep displays uncluttered.

145

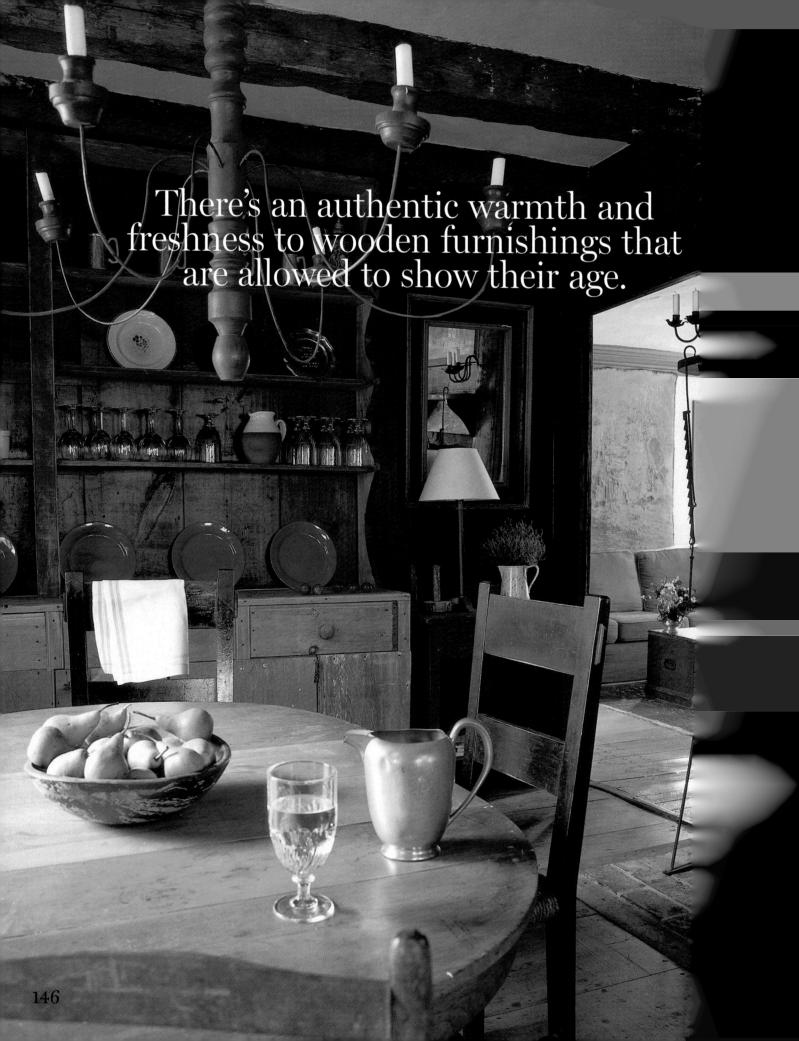

There's an authentic warmth and freshness to wooden furnishings that are allowed to show their age.

146

(Opposite) The owner of this eighteenth-century Nova Scotia home was delighted when, during the renovation, he uncovered original hand-hewn ceiling beams in the eat-in kitchen. A reproduction 1800s candlelight chandelier casts a warm glow over casual evening gatherings. (This page) The traditional grey trim and cheerful yellows in this historic Charlottetown house suggest a formal atmosphere, but the furnishings are pure country casual. The kitchen table, picked up at auction, and the chairs and sideboard all have an Acadian air about them.

details

Use saturated paint shades to recreate an Acadian
mood. • Install wide-plank floorboards and add
simple country antiques and maritime touches —
an old nautical map, a model sailing ship — to
create a suitably weathered atmosphere. • Display
selected pieces of stoneware, pewter, and etched
glassware on the open shelves of a distressed country
cupboard. • Look for one or two evocative old
pieces to anchor each room — for example, an
antique chopping block as an island in the kitchen.

(Opposite, both pictures) A late-nineteenth-century labourer's cottage in Dundas, Ontario, is officially considered an "asymmetrical colonial." Throughout the house, the owners used historic paint colours, wide-plank flooring, and antiques to pull it all together. (This page) Several features in this artfully renovated country kitchen suggest a certain age, but it's the antique chopping block and simple harvest table that really give it a subtle Acadian spin.

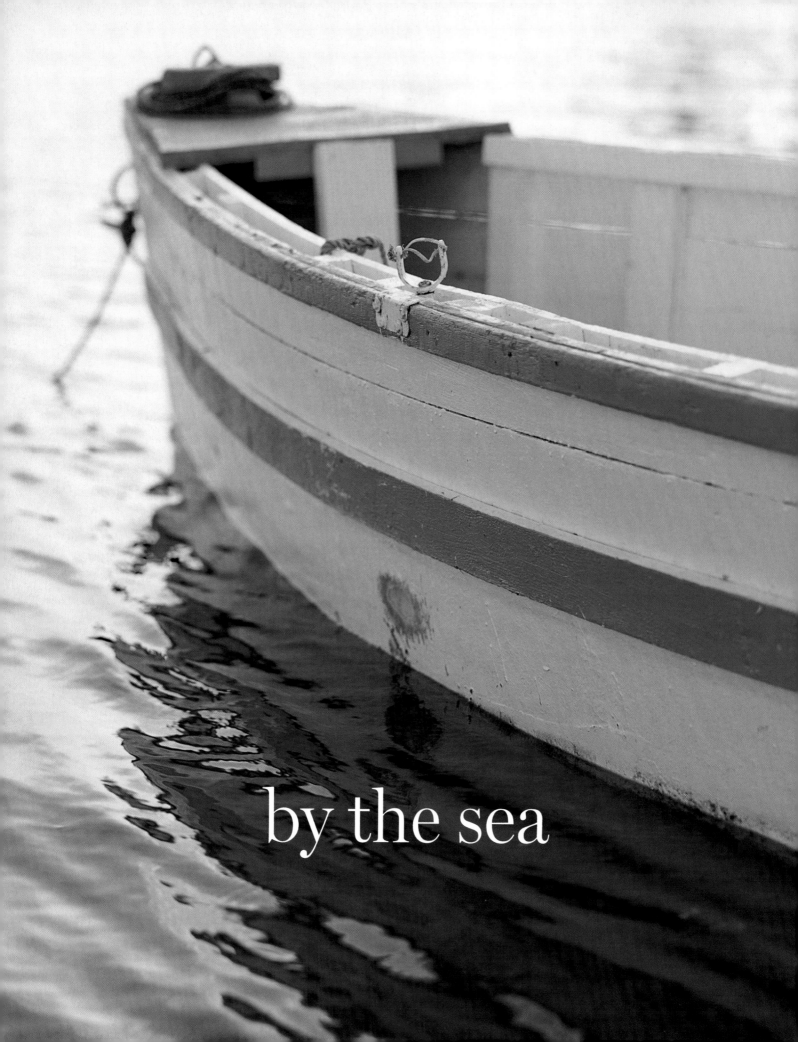

by the sea

Few settings are as evocative as the Canadian seaside. With its compelling combination of elements — sand, water, seashells, sky — and charming motifs, it must surely be one of the most refreshing and inviting sources of decorative inspiration.

As with every country style, there are no hard and fast rules to conjuring up the casual, windswept spirit of the seaside. A few strategic starfish, a model sailing ship, rustic-framed seascapes, an antique wooden lighthouse, and one or two wonderful pieces of naïve folk art are enough to suggest life along Canada's East Coast. The merest hint of crisp blue and white or red and white drives the point home.

A judicious use of nautical references can also achieve the desired effect. Stainless, wall-mounted cleats offer a neat solution to the unsightly drawstrings that dangle from Roman shades. Trim cabinet latches, like those found aboard a sailing vessel, are attractive closures in kitchens and bathrooms. Sailor stripes, nautical collectibles (lanterns, seamen's chests, marine charts), white sailcloth, portraits of ships —

even the novel use of rope as drawer pulls, drapery ties, or rustic trim on pillows — all riff on the seaside conceit.

A successful beachside scheme is not all box-framed sand dollars and driftwood, however. Weathered or bleached floorboards, watery pastels, cobalt blues, and a prodigious use of cream or white are clearly elemental to the airy look. Authentic patterns include checks and ginghams in addition to stripes, faded florals, and quilts. As manufacturers race to embrace the aesthetic, fabrics with marine motifs are becoming more

popular, and there's no use denying their kitschy appeal. Shells, seaweed, fish, sea horses, mermaids, and other sea creatures adorn textiles from some of the world's finest fabric mills. As for floor coverings, braided and hooked rugs that introduce colour and pattern are charming, timeworn choices.

Not even modern dwellings are immune to the seaside's summery appeal. Their decorative interpretations may be more sophisticated and their imagery less literal, but the message is just as clear. A cool, blue-tinged colour scheme, shiny chrome faucets, white pedestal sinks, simple glass drawer pulls, glass mosaic tiles in aqua or sea-blue tones, and a sleek vanity fashioned out of rich walnut wood are all fitting gestures in the modern seaside bathroom. Faux-driftwood flooring and sandy, limestone tiles underscore a beach mood, while fresh white beadboard wainscotting, and glossy painted wood floors work beautifully in both traditional and modern settings.

Décor that evokes the seaside will invariably stir memories of leisurely childhood sojourns, of long, hot days spent scouring the beaches of Nova Scotia, P.E.I., or New Brunswick in search of the buried treasure that eventually made its way into the décor — and consciousness — of landlocked youngsters everywhere. If comfort is fuelled by nostalgia, then decorating by the sea is very comforting indeed.

(Opposite) Weathered floorboards, a range of watery blues, and fresh blue-and-white striping evoke a relaxed, seaside mood. (This page) Memories of endless summer days spent scouring the beach for perfectly shaped shells and other sea treasures fuel our desire to recreate the laidback chic of a beachside retreat.

153

living

As with any country décor, a room inspired by the seaside's compelling elements — sand, sun, water, shells — is open to interpretation. There's the weather-beaten and eclectically furnished beachside shack, the calm and cozy maritime cottage, and the streamlined watery oasis that might, in fact, mask an urban condo.

(Opposite) Although situated by a lake rather than the ocean, there's something about this airy Quebec boathouse that suggests the East Coast. In the living room, old-fashioned wicker furnishings have been rejuvenated with coats of white paint; displays of charming blue-and-white antique plates draw the eye up; and sunny accessories underline the summery mood. (This page) A wooden chair of a certain age, a stack of bold books, and a charming vase of wildflowers are reminiscent of long summer days.

The long association between trim white interior elements and sailing is undeniable.

(Opposite) Serving dishes share space with everyday items on charming open shelves. The pale blue wall peeking out from behind the china and glass offers the mere hint of a seaside inspiration. (This page) This dining room, with its distinctive sofa, fresh blue-and-white colour scheme, and antique armoire is reminiscent of both Swedish country style and an elegant Lunenburg residence. Simple hurricane lamps are the perfect nautical accessory.

details

Bring the outdoors in with an oceanic colour scheme of grey-blue, sand, and soft green. • Splash liberal doses of white everywhere — on beadboard, kitchen cabinets, slipcovers, and window dressings. In a seaside atmosphere, white is an ideal foil. • Heavy up on nautical imagery. Hang pictures of ships, use crisp navy-and-white sailor stripes or rope details, and dig around for shipboard relics: antique hourglasses, binoculars, and old barometers make great accessories.

(Opposite, left) Unpainted windows and wallboards, a reconditioned light, and a sweet trio of flowers have a carefree, timeworn appeal. (Opposite, right) There's a palpable East Coast flavour in this old Ontario cottage. (This page) An inviting daybed, covered in crisp, cottagey pillows, accommodates overnight guests in a quaint lakeside cabin. Rope pulls on its deep storage drawers, and an old chest — with its chipped and peeling paint — add to the seaside illusion.

(This page and opposite) Practical collections of vintage tins and china bring bold colour into two different all-white kitchens. A glassy countertop (this page) recalls a tranquil body of water.

162

eating

Enduring seaworthy colours and materials offer
shortcuts to seaside chic. They also provide a foundation
for a range of practical, welcoming looks. Crisp blue
and white fabrics and china, floorboards and tables the
colour of faded driftwood, and the occasional shot
of bright colour all play well against an aqueous setting.

details

Paint plank walls and kitchen cabinets white and install a gleaming hardwood floor and natural wood trim for a look that's reminiscent of a ship. • Hang pots on a metal rod suspended above the stove. • Use wicker chairs around the dining-room table. But be sure to look for pieces made with hardwood frames and nails; they'll outlast those constructed with staples.

(This page) Together, the tranquillity of blue and purity of white create a refreshing colour combination. Here, the mix adds character to a charming breakfast room. (Opposite) A few novel touches elevate this country kitchen, such as the cabinets faced in chicken wire, a retro-style freestanding stove, and turquoise containers.

(This page) Subtle shades of cool green and a vase of hydrangeas bring the outdoors into this classically appointed bathroom. (Opposite, right) In a guest bedroom, visual interest is ensured by a mix of green tones — all taken from nature.

rest

Even if the sound of water lapping at the
shore is missing from your seaside scenario,
a serene mix of soft shades in the bedroom, a
refreshing spa-like atmosphere in the bathroom,
an arrangement of simple seasonal flowers,
and the occasional beach motif should be
enough to transport you in your dreams.

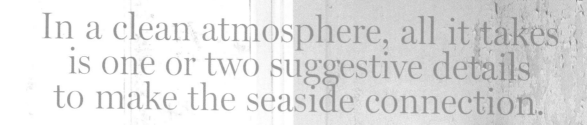

In a clean atmosphere, all it takes
is one or two suggestive details
to make the seaside connection.

(This page) Leaving windows uncovered, even in a bedroom,
is a time-honoured coastal traditional. Here, the trick is
employed in an old Ontario cottage to maximize the
natural light. A green-painted Victorian chest of drawers
provides the only contrast in the simple and serene room.
(Opposite) In a bathroom designed for heavy use, durable
slate floor tiles, white-tiled walls, polished chrome
faucets, double sinks, an adjustable mirror, and ample
storage are the practical considerations. A trio of starfish
and ship-shape door handles are seaworthy accents.

(Both pages) A young boy's nautical-inspired bedroom is a vintage seaside time capsule. A mix of personal photos and beach pictures, an antique bed dressed in layers of white, striped, and quilted bedding, a requisite model sailboat, and the unmistakable combination of blue, white, and red prove the enduring appeal of this scheme. Generations of boys have set sail — at least in their imaginations — in just such a room.

(This page) Tongue-and-groove wainscotting, a vintage claw-foot tub, a porcelain wall-mounted sink with retro faucets, and a sand-coloured bath mat create a country feel with hints of the seaside. (Opposite) Retro hot and cold faucets like those found in old cottages, cool blue soaps, and a happy bunch of daisies suggest summer all year round.

details

Leave windows uncovered for an authentic seaside look. • Pull out all the stops, nautically speaking, when decorating a child's bedroom. Layer the bed in stripes, quilts, and crisp white sheets, hang an old map or seascape, and paint the room blue. • Line up a series of starfish on a bathroom ledge or hang them vertically on the wall. • Old-fashioned fixtures, such as claw-foot tubs, retro chrome faucets, and all-white or pale blue colour schemes contribute to a vintage "by the sea" bathroom.

the french connection

To understand the enormous appeal of this distinctive country style, one only has to consider its evocative origins. The authentic French country home draws inspiration from the romantic landscape that surrounds it. It has its roots in the charming farms, manor houses, village cottages, and rowhouses that dot the French countryside. It respects the integrity of natural materials and draws heavily on the resources of the landscape, particularly stone, walnut, cherry, and oak. It reflects an ingrained respect for traditional arts and crafts.

There is both a layered richness to the French country atmosphere and a pleasing lack of clutter. It has a naturally weathered elegance, and . . . well, it's actually difficult to generalize about this beloved and often refined country style, a perennial favourite among Canadians.

The term *French country* may invoke a very specific image — stone floors, timbered ceilings, rooms filled with lime-rubbed wood and muted shades of beige, taupe, and cream, or conversely, cheery combinations of blue, yellow, and white, and pretty printed fabrics — but there is, in fact, no single decorating style that defines it. Regional differences abound in the French countryside, informing divergent architectural and design elements. In other words, the French country of one province is distinct from that of another. Local construction styles vary widely, too, with limestone façades and terracotta-tiled roofs favoured in the south and half-timbered construction and thatched or slate roofs familiar in the north.

The style's famous interior tones depend largely on regional considerations, too. The northern French country palette is soft and subdued. Everywhere, wooden pieces appear to be washed in a soothing range of almost indescribably gentle colours: soft blues, greens, greys, pinks, puttys, and creams — colours that deepen the farther south you travel. Similarly, though the same kinds of furnishings can be

found across the French countryside, they differ in embellishment and tone of wood — details that depend largely on the native materials at hand and the skill of local craftsmen.

Here in Canada, the quirky charm of French country style finds expression in various interpretations, from the serene colours and textures of stone, sisal, linen, and silk to the sun-bleached flavour of Provence, with its Mediterranean shades of rose, ochre, azure, and soft yellow. Integral to the sunny look are dynamic cotton prints, still inspired today by the pretty-patterned fabrics from India that fed the ports of Southern France in the seventeenth century.

The beauty of this diverse rural design lies in its unique adaptability. An ornately carved armoire with panelled doors or a rustic harvest table — both French country staples — are well suited to a variety of decorating modes. An archetypal display of copper pots dangling from the ceiling or a large limestone hearth imbues a kitchen with an earthy charm. A red-and-white toile boutis, the quintessential French country quilt, works as beautifully at the foot of a traditional four-poster bed as it does draped across a crisp white-slipcovered sofa in a modern country living room. Classic French provincial ladder-back chairs appear at home in both traditional and contemporary Canadian spaces.

Sometimes just one iconic element is enough to evoke a French country aura. Take a chic city apartment, dress its windows with striking drapery panels made of hand-printed Provençal cotton, et voilà. The warmth and spirit of French country style just may soften the long, cold Canadian winter ahead.

(Previous page) A pretty tabletop features flatware unearthed at Paris flea markets. (Opposite) An early twentieth-century dresser set, also hauled back from France, now resides in a Toronto bathroom. (This page) A Quebec dining room demonstrates a pared-down interpretation of polished French country style, mixing muted tones, elegant mirrors, simple glassware, and unfussy furnishings.

At first glance, there's a sunny simplicity to this elegant living room that belies its formal roots. The substantial weight and square lines of the coffee table and the soft tailoring of the sofa are effective foils for the room's more traditional antiques and a charming, wrought-iron chair.

living

It's hard to resist the sunny colours that define
the popular Provençal style, just as it's difficult not to be
seduced by the gentle tones and natural textures
of the country homes to the north. If one can generalize
about French country style, it would be to say that
it's warm, welcoming, and altogether enticing.

Mix natural tones, fine antiques, and rich textures to create formal French country style.

Gothic-arched French doors suggest the obvious in this Toronto living room — a refined but eclectic vision of French country that draws together *bergère* chairs, an antique sideboard, a luxurious leather sofa, a strikingly modern table lamp, and that indispensable country staple — wicker baskets.

(Opposite) There's no mistaking the inspiration in this airy foyer with its arched French doors and natural tones and textures. (This page) Though the owner of this house made the dining-room table of local barnboard, its simple shape and his use of available material is reminiscent of a rustic French country approach. There's a hint of the Old World to the black wrought-iron chairs and chandelier.

(Both pages) The custom-made furnishings in this Montreal kitchen, clearly worthy of a French country home, were designed to complement and even showcase the pretty toile de Jouy wallpaper.

details

Relax the appearance of a formal living room by mixing in contemporary light fixtures and wicker baskets (indispensable for their casual good looks and organizational attributes). • If your home lacks interesting architectural details, add crown moulding or architectural fragments to suggest substance. • Antiques are essential to any formal country room and are most effective when balanced by soft furnishings and contrasting lines. • A woven rush bench — in an entrance hall, living room, or at the foot of the bed — adds a traditional note of charm.

(Opposite) Graphic yet simple dining chairs with caned seats, an antique table, pretty etched glass-ware and diaphanous drapes reflect an appreciation of French country style and taste for simplicity. (This page) A pretty jug, a few branches of pepperberries, and a plate of fresh tomatoes, resting here on the window ledge, bring colour to the monochromatic scheme.

(Opposite) In a farm-inspired kitchen, open shelves display an idiosyncratic assortment of items. A casual dining area features such French accents as strong, warm colours, a spirited mix of fabrics, a touch of romance in the form of a novel chandelier, and a general sense of cozy comfort. Who wouldn't want to savour a meal here?

eating

Is it any wonder that in a country that celebrates good food and drink as France does, the heart of the home would beat in the communal kitchen? An inviting space that accommodates cooking and cleaning areas, and a comfortable place to savour meals is clearly an idea Canadians have warmed to.

Look for similarities in scale, shape, and condition when blending pieces of diverse origin.

This comfortable kitchen is in an old farmhouse
in Ontario's Muskoka lakes district, but take away
the beadboard, and it could just as easily be
found in the French countryside. An old French
gaming table and walnut French country chairs
authenticate the look, whereas the aged cupboard,
repaired and freshly painted, was a local find.

The French make a habit of mixing styles and periods. So do the owners of this cottage in Vancouver's Kitsilano neighbourhood, where the dining room hosts a blend of English antiques, retro collectibles, and French country inspirations — including the scent of lavender wafting in from the garden. A variety of wood tones, French table linens, a pretty upholstery fabric, and a predominance of red account for the room's French country flair.

the french connection

details

For instant French country flavour, use charming toile de Jouy fabric to upholster chairs, paper walls, dress tables or windows, or simply to cover throw cushions. • A French chandelier, or an approximation of one, adds instant atmosphere to a dining room. • Enhance the organic quality of the kitchen with a series of framed botanical prints. • Remove the wooden panels from the front of an antique armoire and replace them with chicken wire.

(Opposite, right) Red-and-white toile overlaid with lace is the foundation for a traditional dining table. (Below) An icon of the style, an intricately carved antique armoire, is faced in chicken wire. (This page) In a newly minted cottage kitchen, French country overtones include the wooden countertops, farmhouse sink, open displays, and cheerful accents.

cottage country

Comfortable. Laidback. Humble. Cozy. The traditional country cottage is a charming retreat — an unassuming structure full of low-maintenance finishes, durable and mostly mismatched furnishings, fresh pretty patterns, and cherished family mementoes. Here, where the pace is unhurried and even chores seem pleasurable, generations of families share time, space, and memories.

For more than a century the romantic notion of cottage living has fired the imaginations of Canadians who hunger for a relaxed getaway and a restored connection to the land. Among weary city-dwellers there can be few ideas as compelling as a weekend or summer home, one far removed from the workaday worries of the city.

The inclination to retreat to a simpler style and slower pace of life may be entirely natural; but to be fair, the roots of cottage living can be traced to eighteenth- and nineteenth-century France and England, where members of the moneyed class saw value and even beauty in the small houses of the working class. These rustic homes, which even then denoted a less complicated, more casual mode of living,

Back in the developing cities, small, efficient homes that fit the cottage ideal were also going up quickly. The essential character of the Arts and Crafts bungalow — a popular style in early-twentieth-century suburbia — was relaxed and cottagey, its commodious porch an invitation to kick-back and watch the world, or at least your neighbours, go by. Inside, the cottage — whether it was by the side of a lake or in the heart of a bustling city — was an intensely personal space. Upholstery fabrics were pale, pretty, and faded with wear. Colours and patterns clashed comfortably. China patterns were busy and mixed for an eclectic display. And an unfussy, practical attitude prevailed.

Remarkably, modern cottage style hasn't strayed far from its rustic origins. Its modest features can still be found as easily in an urban dwelling as by the side of a lake. Welcoming, simple, and undeniably charming, the carefree spirit of early cottage style is still apparent in newer mixes of striped, floral, and checked fabrics. It shows up too in slipcovered furniture or painted wicker chairs and sofas, and in quirky flea market finds, crisp white beadboard, and simple displays of collections.

Cottage style is as always casual, comfortable, and accommodating. It is unpretentious and entirely laidback — suggesting morning coffee and a leisurely crossword one day, and hours of reading and a long paddle the next. But the ultimate test of an inviting atmosphere is its ability to promote the one universal cottage activity: putting your feet up and doing absolutely nothing.

inspired the aristocracy to build modest dwellings on their own estates. At first these were to house members of their staff, but ultimately they became simple getaway cottages for themselves. Since then, the quintessential English country cottage, with its thatched roof, stone walls covered in climbing ivy, winding garden paths and profusion of flowers, has remained a charming symbol of a bucolic way of life.

Here in Canada where the rural terrain is more rugged, early settlers flocked to secluded woods, mountains, and lakes within striking distance of cities in search of an escape from the summer heat. The structures they erected were humble and quirky, with a rustic sense of charm.

(Previous page) This charming cottage, part of a larger estate near London, Ontario, was relocated from elsewhere on the property, renovated, and now serves as a guesthouse. (Opposite) A few vintage cottage accessories. (This page) New drawer pulls and a fresh coat of grey-blue paint recast a tired old chest as a quintessential cottage piece.

living

A home characterized by comfortable, mismatched furnishings, happy clashes of pattern, simple displays of personal collections, and pale, pretty colours is the essence of casual cottage style.

A lifelong collector with a well-trained eye for detail created this airy and inviting beach cottage mood in her rambling Toronto home.

cottage country

(This page, right) Nothing says "cottage" or "relax" as eloquently as a striped canvas hammock, swinging in the breeze. (Below and opposite) Weathered French doors open to allow the outdoors into this picturesque seaside retreat, recently built using reclaimed materials. One quilt conceals a sofabed while another adds charm to an impromptu buffet. Wall-mounted straw hats and old photographs are an expression of the tiny cabin's quirky personality.

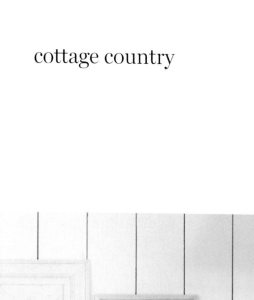

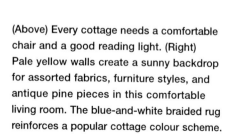

(Above) Every cottage needs a comfortable chair and a good reading light. (Right) Pale yellow walls create a sunny backdrop for assorted fabrics, furniture styles, and antique pine pieces in this comfortable living room. The blue-and-white braided rug reinforces a popular cottage colour scheme.

(This page) This apartment dining room boasts a Scandinavian-style charm. The floor is painted in a striking green-and-white harlequin pattern. The walls are sunny yellow above traditional panelling. A painted toleware chandelier introduces a note of whimsy, and a simple corner cabinet displays treasured china pieces. (Opposite) Small vanities were common in old-fashioned cottages and farmhouses. This one was renewed with fresh coats of paint in two shades, new hardware, and the removal of its original castors.

details

Slipcover tired chairs and sofas with crisp blue-and-white ticking — it never goes out of style. • In a cramped cottage or townhouse, bare floors expand the space visually. • Removing lower cabinet doors and replacing them with a pretty skirt adds instant country flair. • A painted toleware chandelier, typically bursting with random flowers, provides a romantic focal point in a casual dining area. • Add a pegboard at the back entrance to help control the clutter.

The simple, influential style of the authentic cottage kitchen is still being felt today. Double porcelain sinks, skirted lower cabinets, glass-milk pendant lights hung low over the kitchen table, practical plate racks, linoleum flooring — and of course, a spot to eat — all have their place in the modern country kitchen.

eating

(Opposite) A harvest table, decorated simply and paired with a mismatched collection of bare wooden chairs, can accommodate a crowd. (This page) Simple, no-fuss picnics and summer cottages go hand in hand.

(This page) By removing some cabinet doors in this sizable apartment kitchen and painting the backs of the open shelves the same blue as the walls, the owner gained display space. China in cheerful tones brings the room to life. A fanciful tolework chandelier is a funky touch. (Opposite) The only updates to this 1920s cottage kitchen — which now sports a kind of fifties-diner-meets-New England-preppy look — have been achieved with the use of a paintbrush.

Dining *al fresco* on a simply furnished lawn, deck, or patio is the Canadian cottage ideal.

(Opposite) A summer meal taken outdoors is given a fresh spin with an unexpected mint, lavender, and cocoa theme. (This page) A quirky trio of mismatched stools gives family and visiting friends a place to perch in this laidback cottage kitchen. The painted display cabinet is an old hymn-book holder, salvaged from a local church.

details

Dig around flea markets for the kinds of vintage treasures that defined cottage style, circa 1950; they'll give your city home a cottagey flair. • Transform a tired cottage kitchen with a fresh coat of paint, new hardware, pendant lights, and some additional open shelving to show off your collections. • Use pretty sea-washed shades of turquoise, aqua, and greenish-grey to suggest an ocean or lakeside location.

(Opposite) Colourful flea market finds and a small spray of ranunculus recall an innocent era in the sunny breakfast nook of this Montreal flat. (This page) The charmingly kitschy breakfast setting includes Pyrex pieces in spring pastels, Bakelite cutlery, and a vintage fruit-patterned tablecloth.

rest

Few things rival an afternoon nap in a cottage
bedroom — a room devoted purely to sleep.
It's hard not to slumber when you're tucked under
a cotton quilt softened by years of use and hand
washing, lulled by the sound of waves lapping
against the shore, and warmed by the sun filtering
through curtains that waft in the gentle breeze...

(Opposite) An old cast-iron bed and a child's play table give this city bedroom an unmistakably cottagey vibe. (This page) A cheerful mix of linens — mainly florals, stripes, and checks — prove that patterns needn't match if their colours do.

(This page) A few favourite items adorn a simple country "headboard." Crisp white sheets allow two favourite quilts to take centre stage. (Opposite) After the bed, a chest of drawers is a country bedroom's most pivotal piece. These two charmers carry it off in classic cottage style.

Subtly aged surfaces introduce a sense of history. Weathered wood, vintage fabrics, and timeworn metals all point to the passage of time.

(This page) Cottage bedrooms are often called upon to accommodate guests. Bunks are an obvious solution, but a row of single beds, each one dressed with different quilts and bed linens, offers a pretty alternative. (Opposite) Striking red accents and an inviting mix of old and new contribute to this guest room's subtle drama.

details

When dressing a bed in a variety of patterns, stick to a consistent colour palette. • Flea markets and second-hand stores are great sources of furnishings for cottage bedrooms, or those you'd like to look cottagey. The inherent character and low cost of items you'll find there make them perfect for filling up rooms inexpensively. • Don't worry if your ancestors weren't crafty. You can create an instant cottage atmosphere with a newly minted, old-fashioned-looking quilt.

directory

The following is but a small selection of the many wonderful sources available to Canadians wanting to create their own country-style havens.

The Farm Revisited

Furniture and Accessories

Country Furniture
Vancouver, BC.
(604) 738-6411, (604) 985-3359
www.countryfurniture.com

Hardware
Toronto, ON.
(416) 462-3099

Woodcraft
Markham, ON.
(plus 3 other locations)
(905) 475-2488
www.woodcraft.ca

Lighting

Turn of the Century Lighting
Toronto, ON.
(416) 362-6203
www.tocl.on.ca

Reclaimed Materials

Artefacts Salvage & Design
(519) 664-3760
www.artefacts.ca

Balleycanoe & Co.
Mallorytown, ON.
www.balleycanoe.com

Flooring

Historic Lumber
(519) 853-0008
www.historiclumber.ca

K&I Pine Flooring
Collingwood, ON.
(705) 445-0122

West Lincoln Barnboard & Beams Ltd.
(800) 719-9051
www.antiquewoods.com

Architecture

John Robert Carley
Toronto, ON.
(416) 481-6889
(See pp. 17,149)

Northern Light

Furniture and Accessories

Au Lit Homestyle
Toronto, ON.
(416) 489-7010
(800) 363-6080

The Cross
Vancouver, BC.
(604) 689-2900
www.thecrossdesign.com

Liberty
Vancouver, BC.
(604) 682-7499
www.libertyinside.com

Peridot
Vancouver, BC.
(604) 736-4499
www.peridot.ca

Stacaro
Toronto (416) 367-5959
Montreal (514) 287-9800
www.stacaro.com

White on White
St. Catharines, ON.
(905) 685-0111
www.whiteonwhite.ca

White Space Interiors
(866) 890-2764
www.whitespace-interiors.com

Spirit of the West

Furniture and Accessories

Restoration Hardware
(416) 322-9422
www.restorationhardware.com

Harvest House Furniture for Life
Schomberg, ON.
(888) 241-9960
www.harvesthouse.ca

Architect

Keith Jakobsen
Jakobsen Associates
Vancouver, BC.
(604) 261-5619
www.jakobsenassociates.com
(See pp. 116,117)

New England

Furniture and Accessories

Putti Fine Furnishings
Toronto, ON.
(416) 972-7652
(800) 649-3120

Rousseau's
Whitby, ON.
(905) 668-3483
(800) 387-0242
www.rousseaus.ca

Design Services, Custom Furniture and Textiles

Julia West Home
Toronto, ON.
(415) 927-1502
(800) 300-9390
www.juliawesthome.com

Custom Lampshades

Birds of Paradise
Toronto, ON.
(416) 366-4067
www.bopl.on.ca

Paint and Wallpaper

Farrow & Ball
(877) 363-1040
www.farrow-ball.com

Appliances

AGA
Northern Pacific
Appliance Distributing
Burnaby, BC.
(800) 663-8686
www.bellevie.ca

Antiques and Collectibles

Cynthia Findlay Antiques
Toronto, ON.
(416) 260-9057
www.cynthiafindlay.com

Drapery Hardware and Metalwork

Steptoe™ & Wife Antiques Limited
Restoration Products
Toronto, ON.
www.steptoewife.com

Urban Country

Furniture and Accessories

Bacci's
Vancouver, BC.
(604) 733-4933

Commute Home
Toronto, ON.
(416) 861-0521
www.commutehome.com

The Finnish Place
Toronto, ON.
(416) 222-7575
(877) 346-7467
www.finnishplace.com

Hollace Cluny
Toronto, ON.
(416) 968-7894

Montauk
Vancouver, Calgary,
Toronto, Montreal
www.montauksofa.com

Pottery Barn
Toronto, Vancouver
www.potterybarn.ca

Sarah Richardson Design
www.sarahrichardsondesign.com

Style Garage
Toronto, ON.
(416) 534-4343
www.stylegarage.com

By the Sea

Furniture and Accessories

Caban
Toronto, Vancouver,
Montreal, Calgary
www.caban.com

Martha Stewart Everyday
Sears across Canada
(800) 267-3277
www.sears.ca

Nitty Gritty Reproductions
Toronto, ON.
(416) 364-1393
www.nittygritty.ca

Antiques

Blue Pump
Toronto, ON.
(416) 944-1673

The French Connection

Furniture and Accessories

Arthur Quentin
Montreal, PQ.
(514) 843-7513
www.arthurquentin.com

French Country
Toronto, ON.
(416) 944-2204

Moutarde
Outremont, PQ.
(514) 272-1212

Trianon
Toronto, ON.
(416) 363-9851
www.trianon-online.com

Interior Design

Lori Morris Designs
Toronto, ON.
(416) 972-1515

Antiques

Kantelberg Antiques
Toronto, ON.
(416) 964-0192
www.kantelbergantiques.com

Fireplace Mantels

Historical Building Materials
Etobicoke, ON.
(416) 784-9244
www.rdfabbricati.com

Cottage Country

Furniture and Accessories

April Cornell
www.aprilcornell.com

Lola Home & Apparel
Vancouver, BC.
(604) 633-5017

Martha Stewart Everyday
Sears across Canada
(800) 267-3277
www.sears.ca

Vie de Campagne
Westmount, PQ.
(514) 484-2199

Antiques and Collectibles

Antiques at Hyde Park
London, ON.
(519) 472-0322

Elora Antique Market
Elora, ON.
(800) 393-8715

Appliances

Elmira Stoveworks
Elmira, ON.
www.elmirastoveworks.com

acknowledgments

Many people were instrumental in creating this book. Thank you to Ann Marie Favot for her organizational prowess, Elisa McLellan for her artful production expertise, Carol Moskot for her design inspiration, Pamela Erlichman for her unerring eye, Suzanne Moutis for her thoughtful feedback, Gloria Wilkinson for her cheerful administrative aid, Alice Unger for making it look so great, and Tom Hopkins for his valuable guidance. Thank you also to Nils, Bronwyn, and Hans.

There are three groups of people without whom this book simply wouldn't exist. And so we'd like to thank:

The photographers, whose pictures bring to life the warmth and vitality of Canadian country style: Janet Bailey p. 137; Simon Bevan pp. 80, 83, 154, 155, 202 (below), 203; Stacey Brandford pp. 29, 31, 92, 93, 98 (top), 134, 189 (right), 194, 206, 210, 216; Evan Dion pp. 9, 46, 159, 160 (right), 168, 190, 191; Yvonne Duivenvoorden pp. 20, 21, 24, 28 (left), 30 (left), 35 (below), 36, 38, 39, 50, 51, 82, 103, 119, 124, 130, 145 (right), 147, 150, 153, 179, 207, 208, 209; Donna Griffith pp. 16, 19, 22, 23, 32, 33, 34, 40, 41, 42, 43, 44, 45, 48, 52, 53, 54, 55, 56, 57, 58, 59, 66, 67, 70, 73, 74, 84 (right), 85, 88, 89, 97, 102 (below), 114, 115, 118 (top and bottom), 125 (left), 126, 127, 128, 138, 139, 140, 141, 144, 145, 148, 157, 160 (left), 161, 162, 164, 165, 169, 170, 171, 172, 173, 177, 178, 182, 184, 185, 186, 187, 198, 199, 202 (above), 204 (left), 212, 217, 219, 220, 221; Gabor Jurina p. 211; Per Kristiansen pp. 47, 49, 84 (left); Virginia Macdonald pp. 17, 30 (right), 86, 87, 95, 96, 98 (bottom), 100, 101, 143, 149, 188; Rob Melnychuk pp. 14, 18, 72, 106, 107, 110, 111, 116, 117, 192, 193; Robert Pelletier pp. 204, 205, 213, 218; Jonathan Savoie pp. 60, 63, 69, 76, 77; Robin Stubbert pp. 94 (below), 135; Martin Tessler pp. 12, 62, 64, 65, 68, 78, 79, 92, 93; Debra Thier pp. 27, 28 (right), 35 (above), 71, 75, 90, 94 (top), 99, 102 (top), 104, 108, 109, 112, 113, 120, 121, 122, 123, 131, 132, 133, 136, 146, 152, 156, 163, 166, 167, 174, 176, 180, 181, 183, 189 (left), 195, 196, 214, 215; Andreas Trauttmansdorff pp. 142, 158, 200, 201; James Tse p. 26; George Whiteside pp. 8, 91; Ted Yardwood pp. 15, 25, 125 (right, above, and below).

The contributing designers and stylists whose creative talent energizes these pages and that of the magazine: Heather Cameron, Joan Mackie, Nicola Marc, Carrie McCarthy, Lara McGraw, Sarah Richardson, Thomas Smythe, Lynn Spence, and Julia West.

And of course, **the homeowners** from coast to coast who have generously allowed us to photograph their homes. We couldn't have done it without them.

Front cover details: Daybed and room design by Sarah Richardson Design.

Erin McLaughlin is the Editor of *Canadian Home & Country* magazine. For more than four years, Erin and her team of editors have been defining Canadian country style for décor-loving Canadians. Erin grew up in a household of design aesthetes and has had a lifelong passion for decorating and design. She has completed extensive renovations on two homes in Toronto, most recently refurbishing a heritage Victorian rowhouse in the downtown core.

Jennifer David is a writer and editor who lives in Toronto. She writes frequently about design and is a regular contributor to a number of magazines, including *Canadian Home & Country*.